All-time hits from Latin America for B♭ clarinet and piano

Succès de toujours d'Amérique latine pour clarinette en si bémol et piano
Unvergängliche Hits aus Südamerika für Klarinette in B und Klavier

arranged by Alan Gout

CONTENTS

© 1997 by Faber Music Ltd
First published in 1997 by Faber Music Ltd
3 Queen Square London WC1N 3AU
Music set by Woodrow Edition
Cover illustration by Lynette Williamson
Printed in England by Caligraving Ltd
All rights reserved

ISBN 0-571-51772-2

To buy Faber Music publications or to find out about the full
range of titles available please contact your local music retailer
or Faber Music sales enquiries:

Tel: +44 (0)1279 82 89 82
Fax: +44 (0)1279 82 89 83
sales@fabermusic.com
www.fabermusic.com

1. Mambo Jambo

Perez Prado

4

2. Mexican Hat Dance

Trad.

3. La Cucaracha

Trad.

4. Habañera

Georges Bizet

Allegretto quasi andantino

5. La Cumparsita

Rodriguez

6. La Paloma

Sebastián Yradier

7. The Girl from Ipanema

Antonio Carlos Jobim

* Countermelody. Improvise or compose your own if you wish (6 bars).

8. Tico Tico

Zequinha Abreu

9. Adios

Enric Madriguera

30

The 'PLAY' Series

from Faber Music

Play Ballads (flute and piano)	ISBN 0-571-52002-2
Play Ballads (clarinet and piano)	ISBN 0-571-51999-7
Play Ballads (alto saxophone and piano)	ISBN 0-571-52008-1
Play Ballads (trumpet and piano)	ISBN 0-571-51996-2
Play Cabaret (C instruments and piano)	ISBN 0-571-51017-5
Play Gershwin (violin and piano)	ISBN 0-571-51622-X
Play Gershwin (cello and piano)	ISBN 0-571-51623-8
Play Gershwin (clarinet and piano)	ISBN 0-571-51754-4
Play Gershwin (alto saxophone and piano)	ISBN 0-571-51755-2
Play Jazztime (violin and piano)	ISBN 0-571-51908-3
Play Jazztime (flute and piano)	ISBN 0-571-51822-2
Play Jazztime (clarinet and piano)	ISBN 0-571-51821-4
Play Jazztime (alto saxophone and piano)	ISBN 0-571-51909-1
Play Jazztime (trumpet and piano)	ISBN 0-571-52045-6
Play Latin (piano)	ISBN 0-571-51895-8
Play Latin (flute and piano)	ISBN 0-571-51771-4
Play Latin (clarinet and piano)	ISBN 0-571-51772-2
Play Latin (alto saxophone and piano)	ISBN 0-571-52047-2
Play Latin (trumpet and piano)	ISBN 0-571-52046-4
Play Showtime (cello and piano)	ISBN 0-571-51851-6
Play Showtime Book 1 (violin and piano)	ISBN 0-571-51588-6
Play Showtime Book 2 (violin and piano)	ISBN 0-571-51530-4
Play Showtime Book 1 (alto saxophone and piano)	ISBN 0-571-51616-5
Play Showtime Book 2 (alto saxophone and piano)	ISBN 0-571-51606-8
Play Showtime Book 1 (trumpet and piano)	ISBN 0-571-51615-7
Play Showtime Book 2 (trumpet and piano)	ISBN 0-571-51605-X

FABER ff MUSIC

Welcome to …

Paul Harris's
Clarinet Basics

A method for individual and group learning

Clarinet Basics is a landmark method by one of the leading figures in clarinet education. It starts at absolute beginner level and progresses to about Grade 2 level. The method is set out in 22 stages, each of which includes:

- a wonderful variety of concert pieces from the great composers

- traditional tunes and fun, original exercises

- 'finger gyms' and 'warm ups' to help establish a sound technique

- invaluable 'fact files' and 'quizzes' to teach notation and general musicianship

- helpful, clear 'fingering charts' and 'rhythm boxes'

- great illustrations!

The separate teacher's book contains clarinet and piano accompaniments, suggestions for group work and teaching tips.

Clarinet Basics (pupil's book) ISBN 0-571-51814-1
Clarinet Basics (teacher's book) ISBN 0-571-51815-X

Also available:
Andy Hampton's Saxophone Basics
Pupil's book ISBN 0-571-51972-5   Teacher's book ISBN 0-571-51973-3